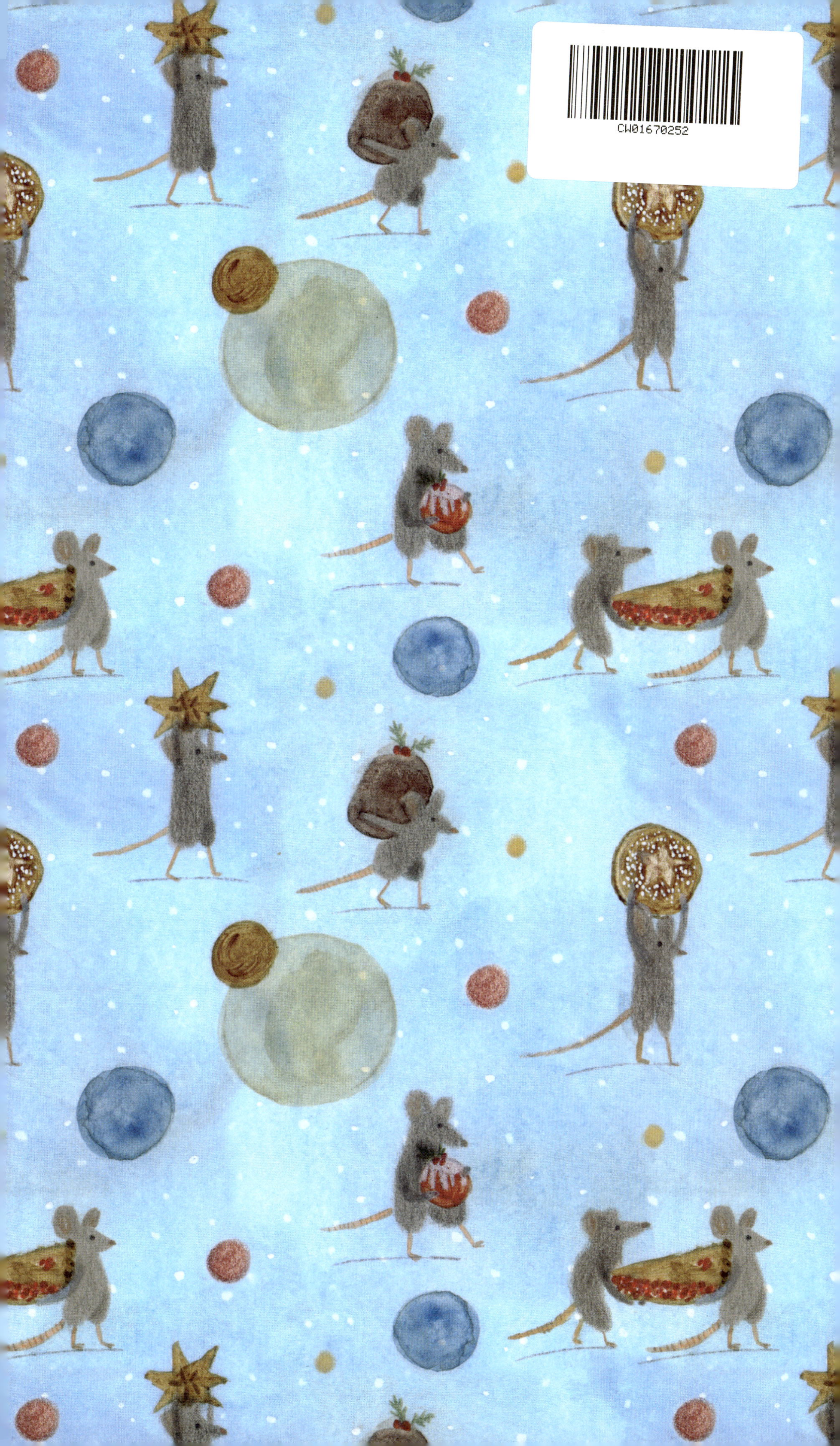

Henry and the Lion's Christmas Feast

Joseph Coelho

Vivien Mildenberger

Chatsworth

Henry and the Lion's Christmas Feast

ISBN: 978-1-91619-269-0

First published 2024

Printed in the UK by Northend

Publisher

Chatsworth House Trust & Chatsworth Estate Trading Limited

Estate Office, Edensor, Bakewell, Derbyshire, England DE45 1PP

Chatsworth House Trust is a charity registered in England and Wales No. 511149, Company No. 1541046

A percentage of every book sale is donated to the charity to help preserve Chatsworth for everyone to enjoy, and to fund our learning and community programmes.

chatsworth.org

MIX
Paper | Supporting responsible forestry
FSC FSC® C019447

Who is Henry?

Henry Cavendish was the grandson of the 2nd Duke of Devonshire and a renowned scientist active in the late 1700s. Although extremely shy and rigidly routine-driven, he made significant contributions to scientific research, including the discovery of hydrogen, and earned the nickname "the man who weighed the world" for his experiment to determine the Earth's density. Despite limited social interactions, his meticulous experiments and correspondence with leading scientists such as Benjamin Franklin and William Herschel highlighted his genius, leading to posthumous comparisons to Isaac Newton.

Joseph Coelho

Joseph Coelho is a best-selling, multi-award winning children's playwright and author of over 45 books. His *The Boy Lost in The Maze* was the winner of the 2024 *Carnegie Medal* for writing and has received international acclaim appearing on the White Raven Book list - Munich, The IBBY UK Honour Books List and awarded The Extraordinary Book of 2023 by The International Children's Literature Festival of Berlin. Joseph was the Waterstone's Children's Laureate 2022 - 2024.

Vivien Mildenberger

Vivien Mildenberger is an award winning illustrator based in Nashville, Tennessee. She has illustrated numerous children's books including *Comet Chaser, All in a Drop* and her upcoming author/illustrated debut *Otto and the Story Tree.*

Her creativity and technical skill has earned her numerous awards and accolades including the American Library Association's Sibert Honor Book, as well as appearing in the World Illustration Awards, American Illustration, New American Paintings and many others.

Little Henry Cavendish
has heard there's a lion
at Chatsworth House.
From an old dusty book he reads...

"The Chatsworth Lion
has a terrible roar
and terrible claws
on his terrible paws.

He skulks down the corridors
of this massive old house
squeezes under each doorway
because he's the size of...

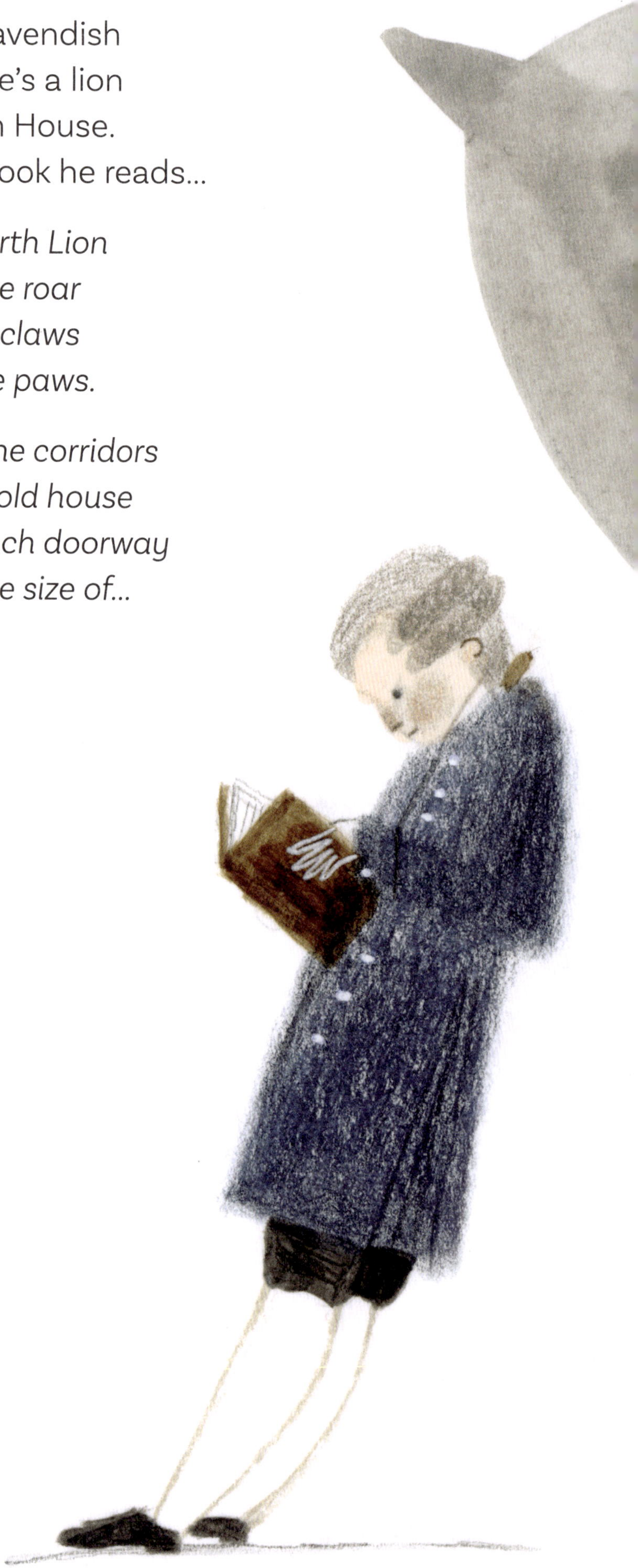

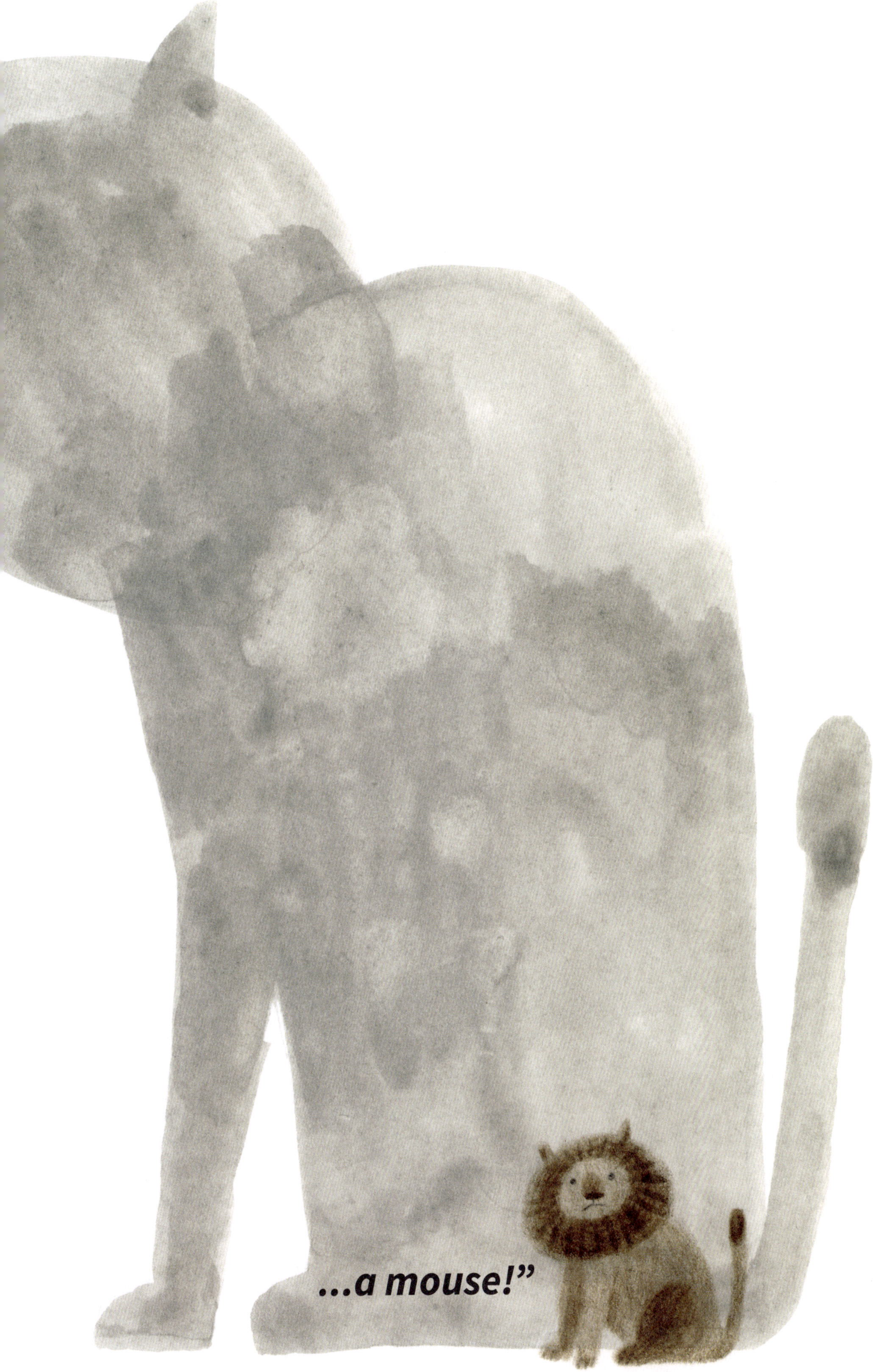

...a mouse!"

But Henry's a scientist
he questions everything he sees...
the nature of air,
the secrets of geology.

He has no time for fantasy,
Henry doesn't believe in the beast.
He has experiments to complete,
before the Christmas midnight feast.

For there's a Christmas meal tonight
and Lion wants to go too
but Lion has no invitation
What's a little lion to do?

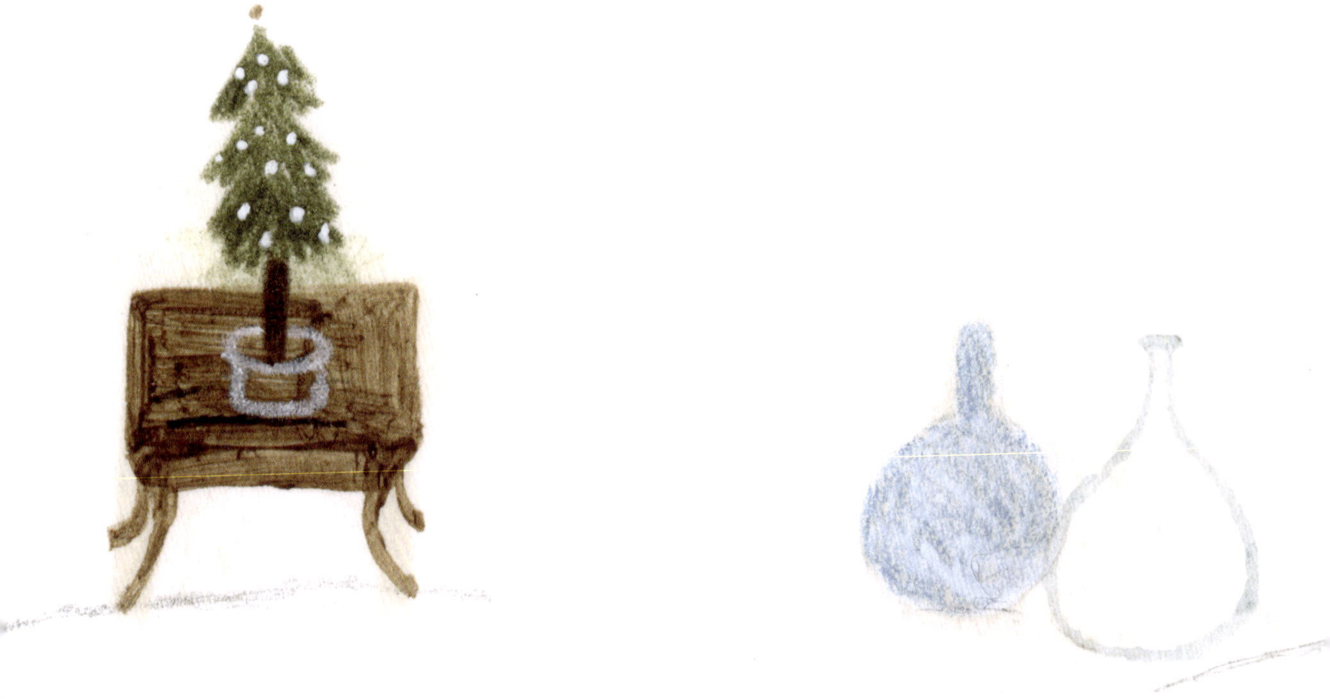

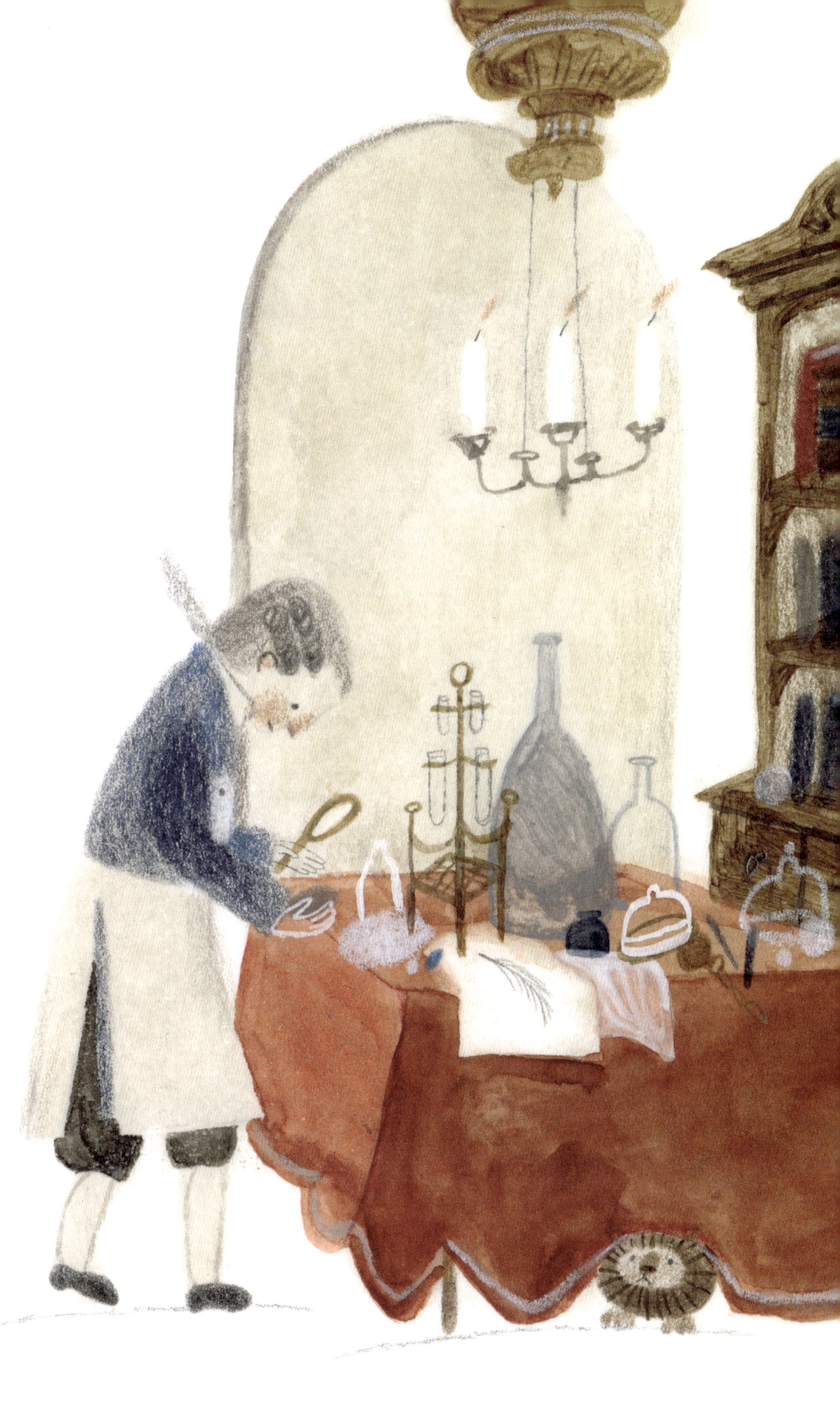

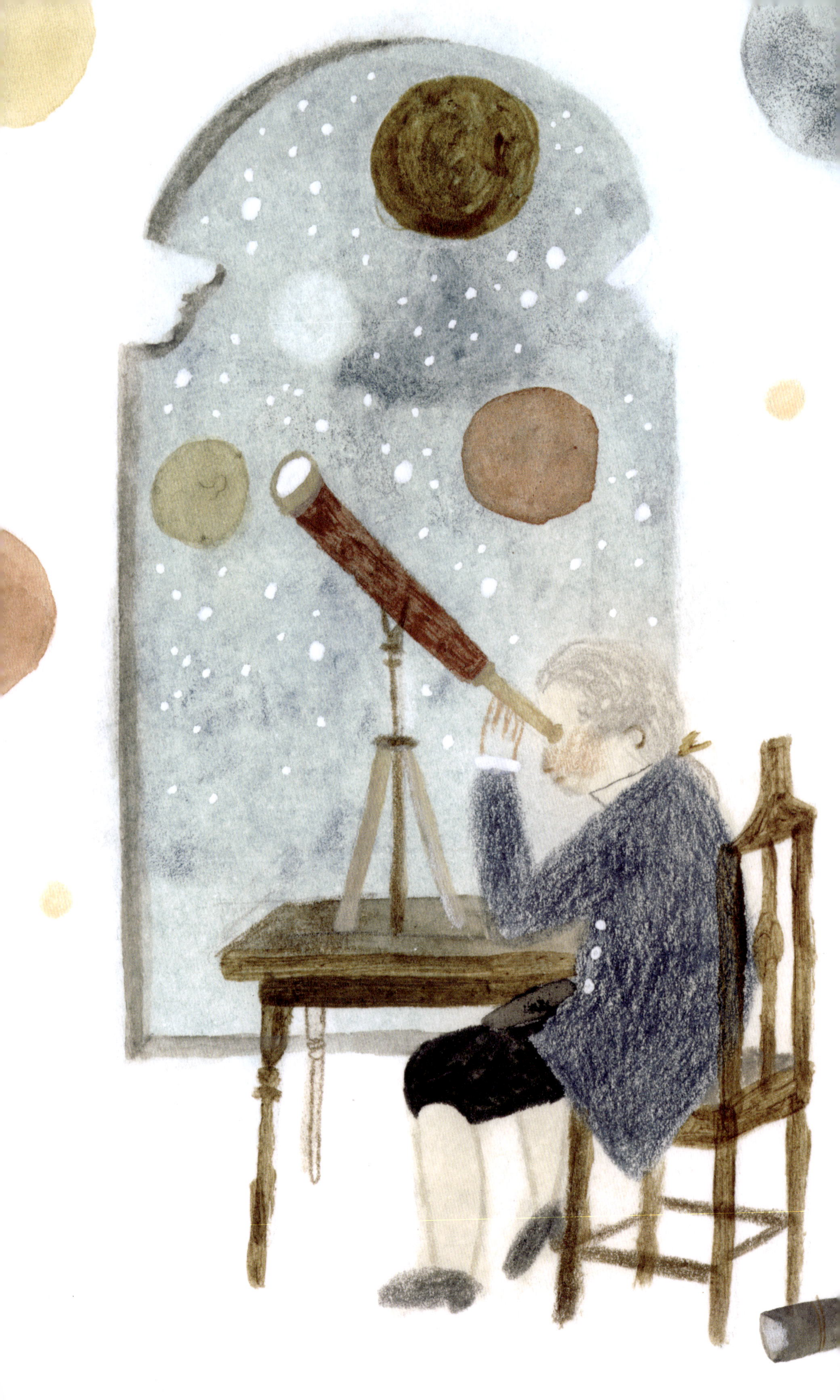

Henry doesn't notice Lion
so small and ever so tiny.
Henry's searching for Venus...

"Ooooh so round and shiny!"

When Henry's not looking
Lion "borrows" a telescope
"I'll spy a way to the feast,"
he says, drooling with hope.

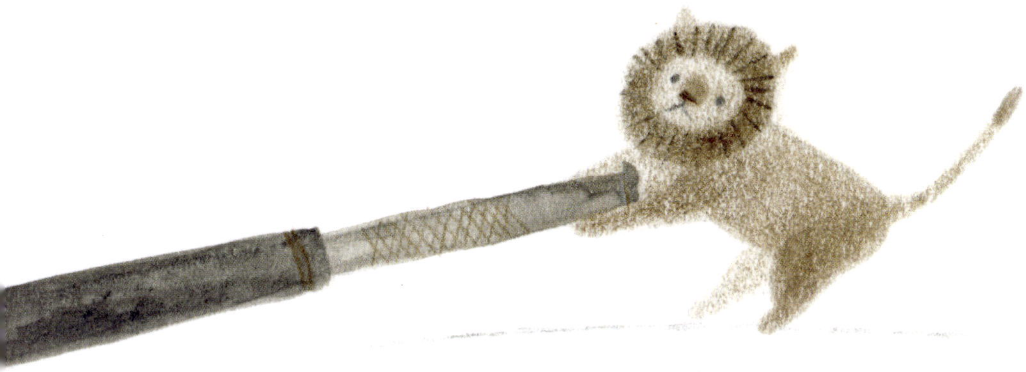

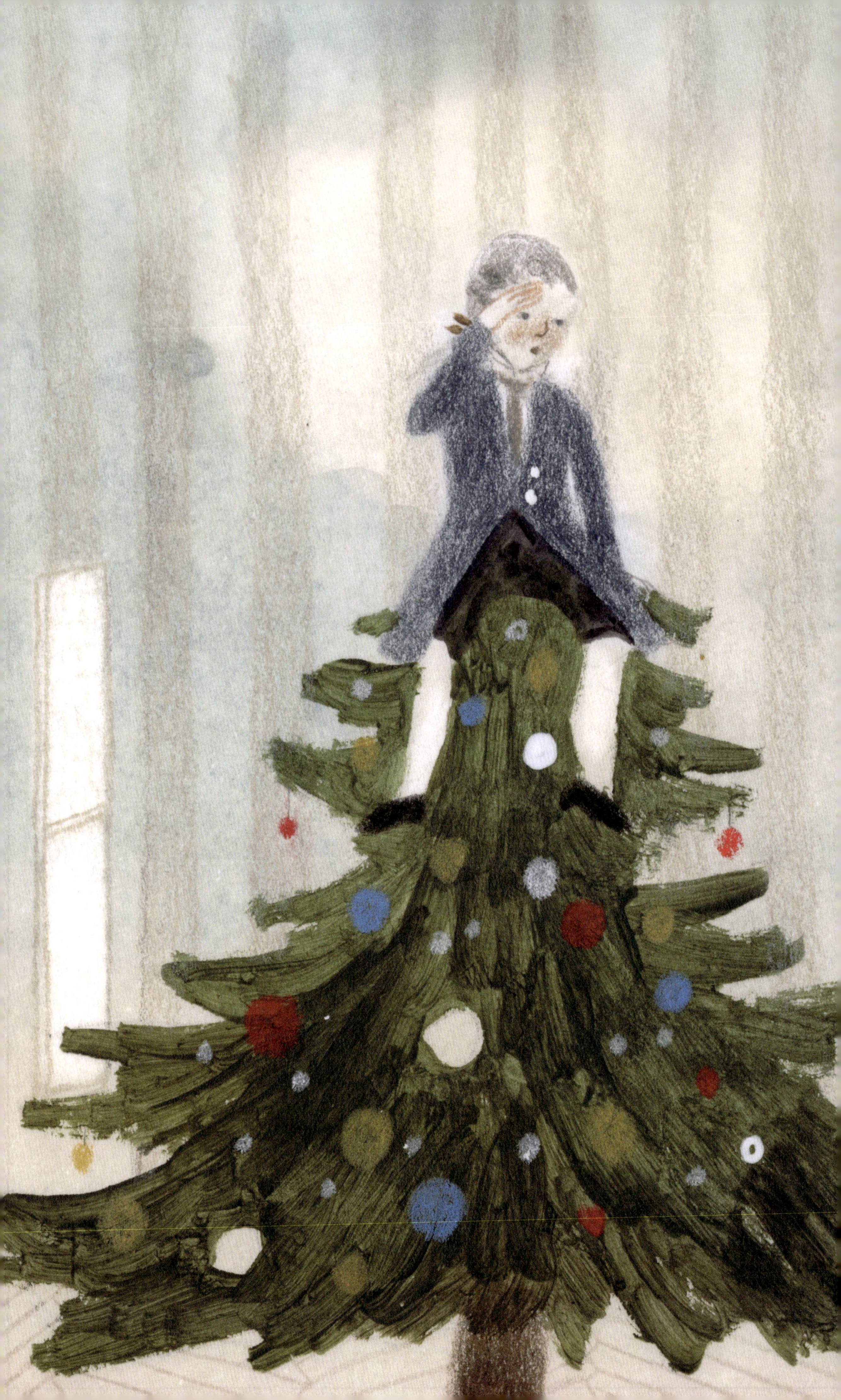

"My telescope is missing!
where could it be?"

Henry searches high
from atop his Christmas tree.

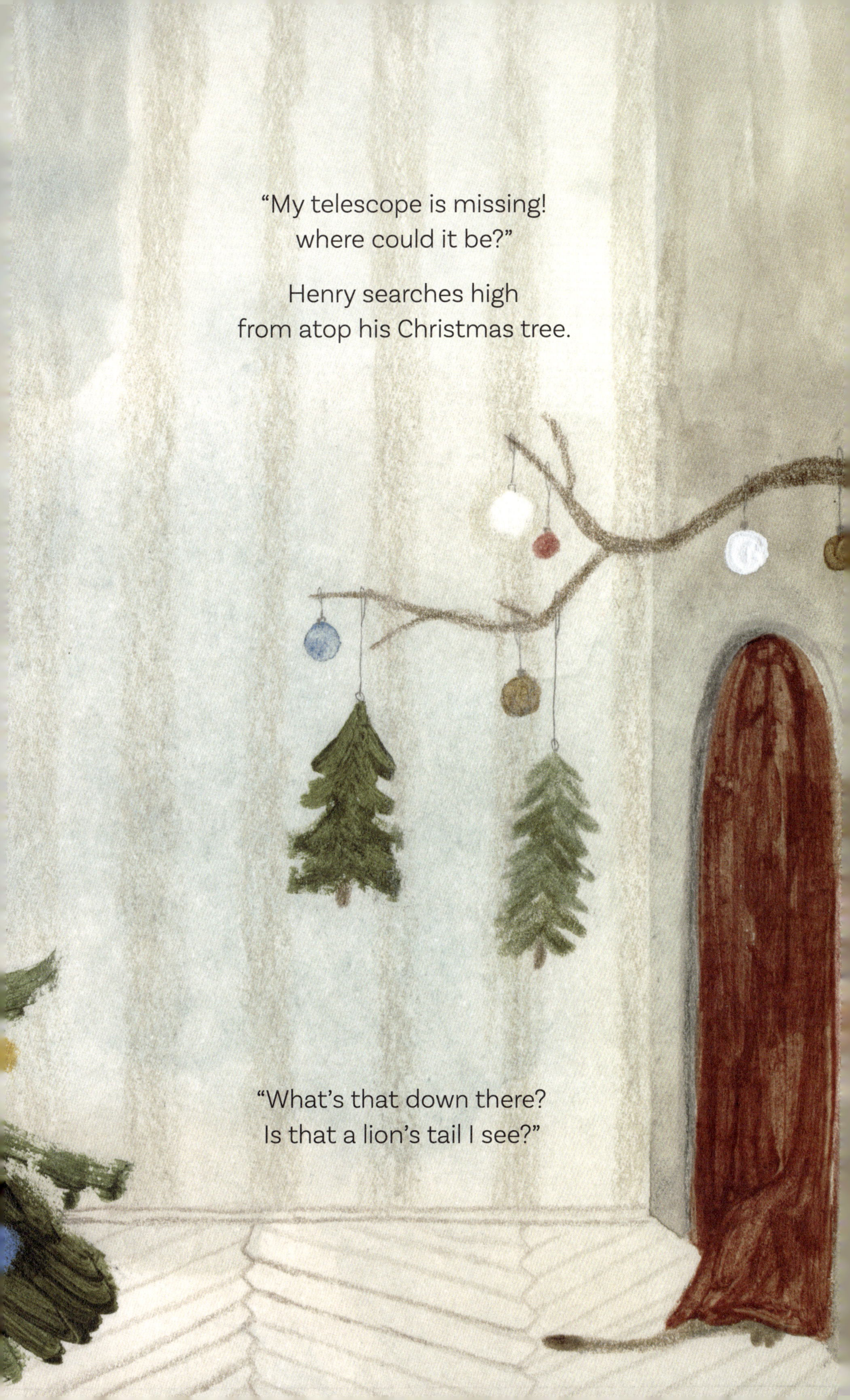

"What's that down there?
Is that a lion's tail I see?"

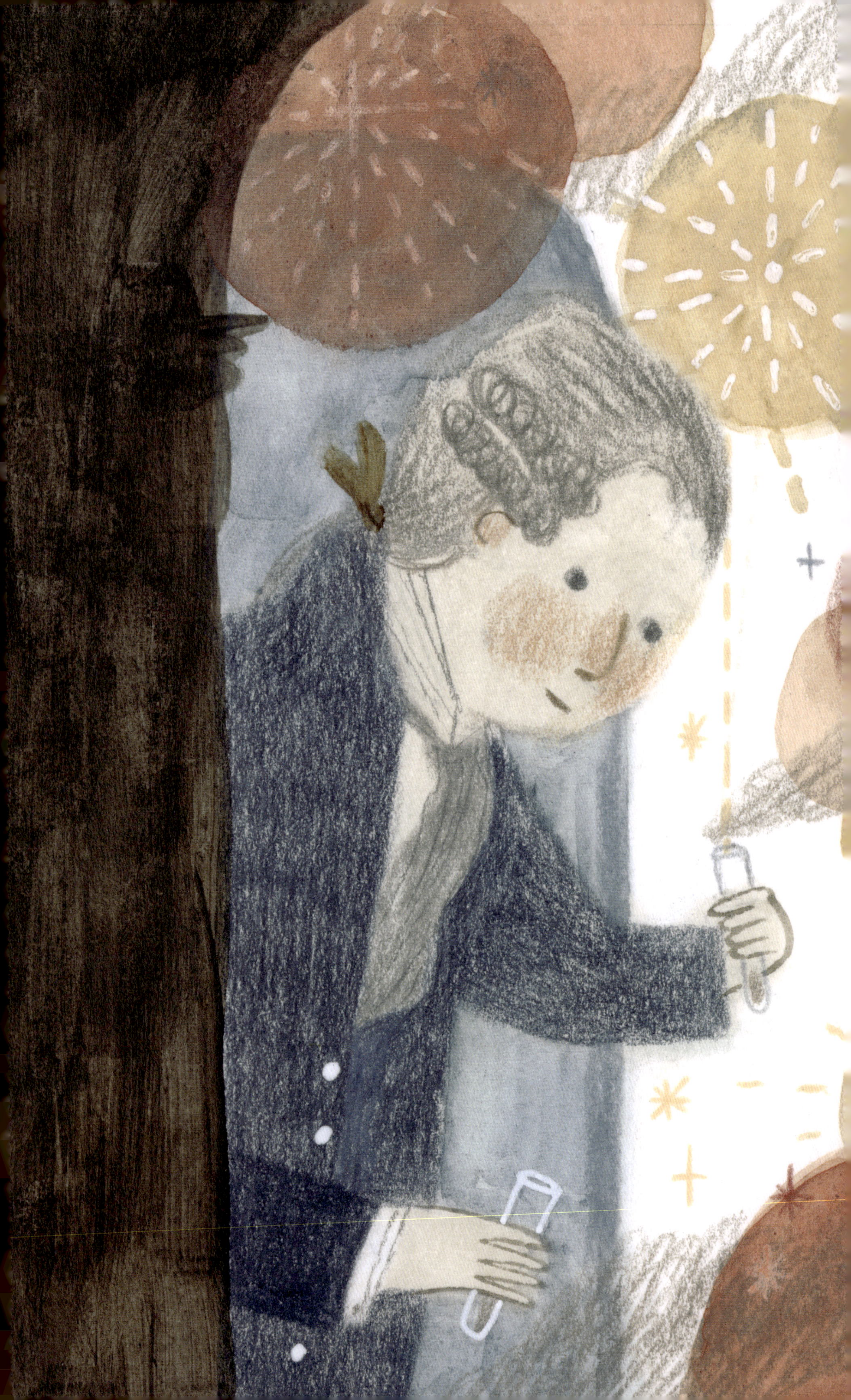

Henry uses science
to make sparks in the air
"By lighting up hydrogen
I'll give that lion a scare!"

There are BANGS! and
there are POPS!
that give little Lion a fright
he leaps out into the open
to Henry's cunning delight!

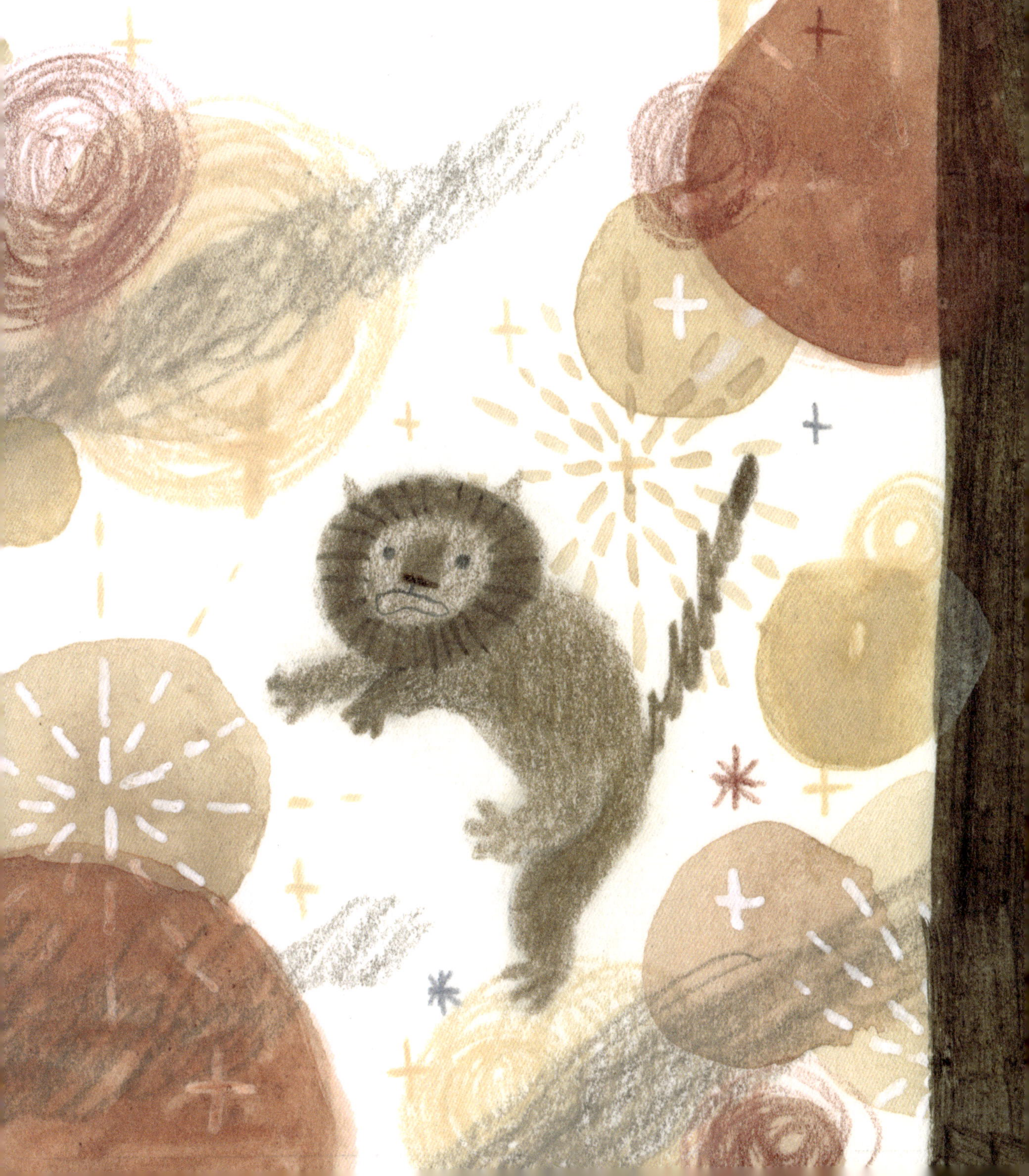

"I've found the Chatsworth Lion!"

Little Henry cries out
but he's not happy for long...

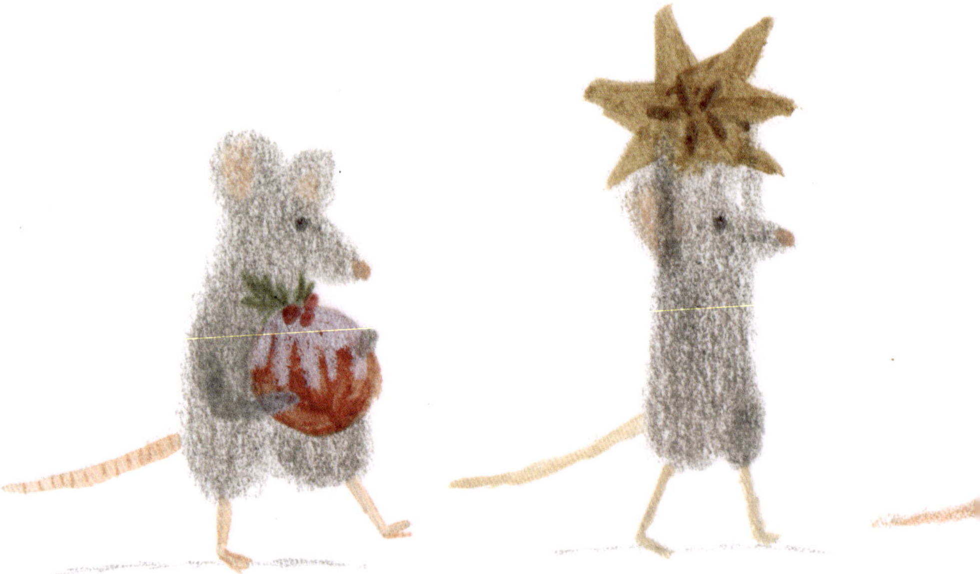

A menace of mice
scurry about!

They leap and they dive
they are clever little beasts.

“Help me catch the mice,” Says Henry,
“and I’ll invite you to the feast!”

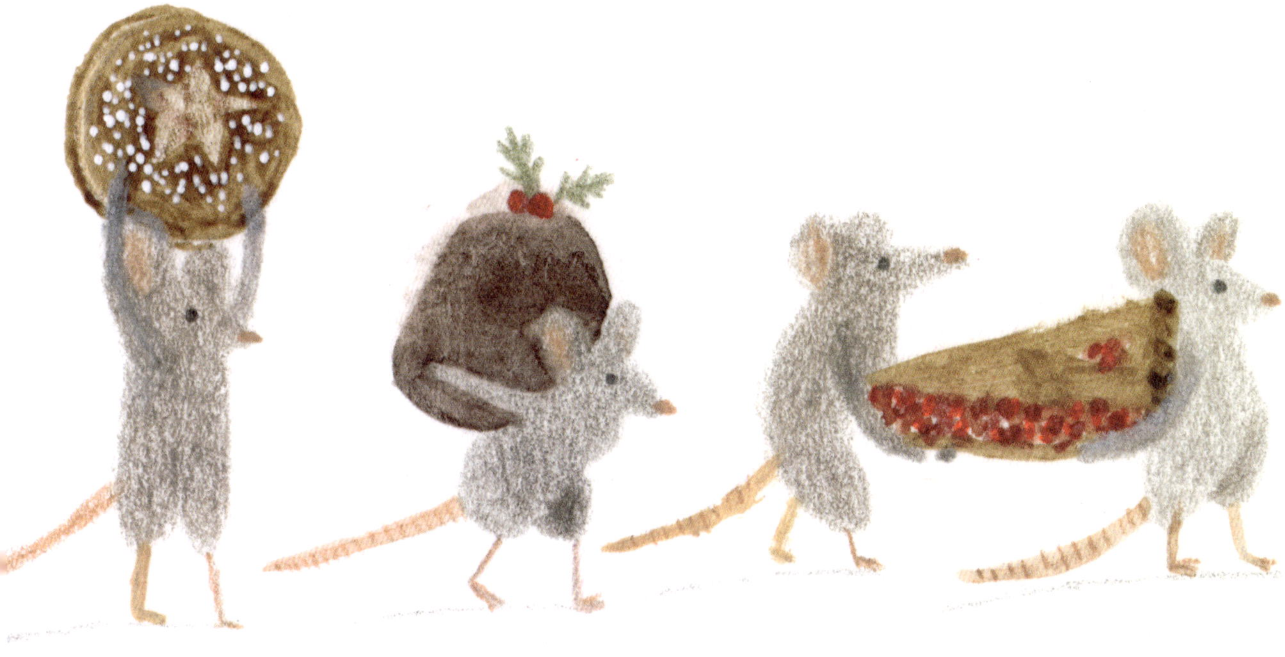

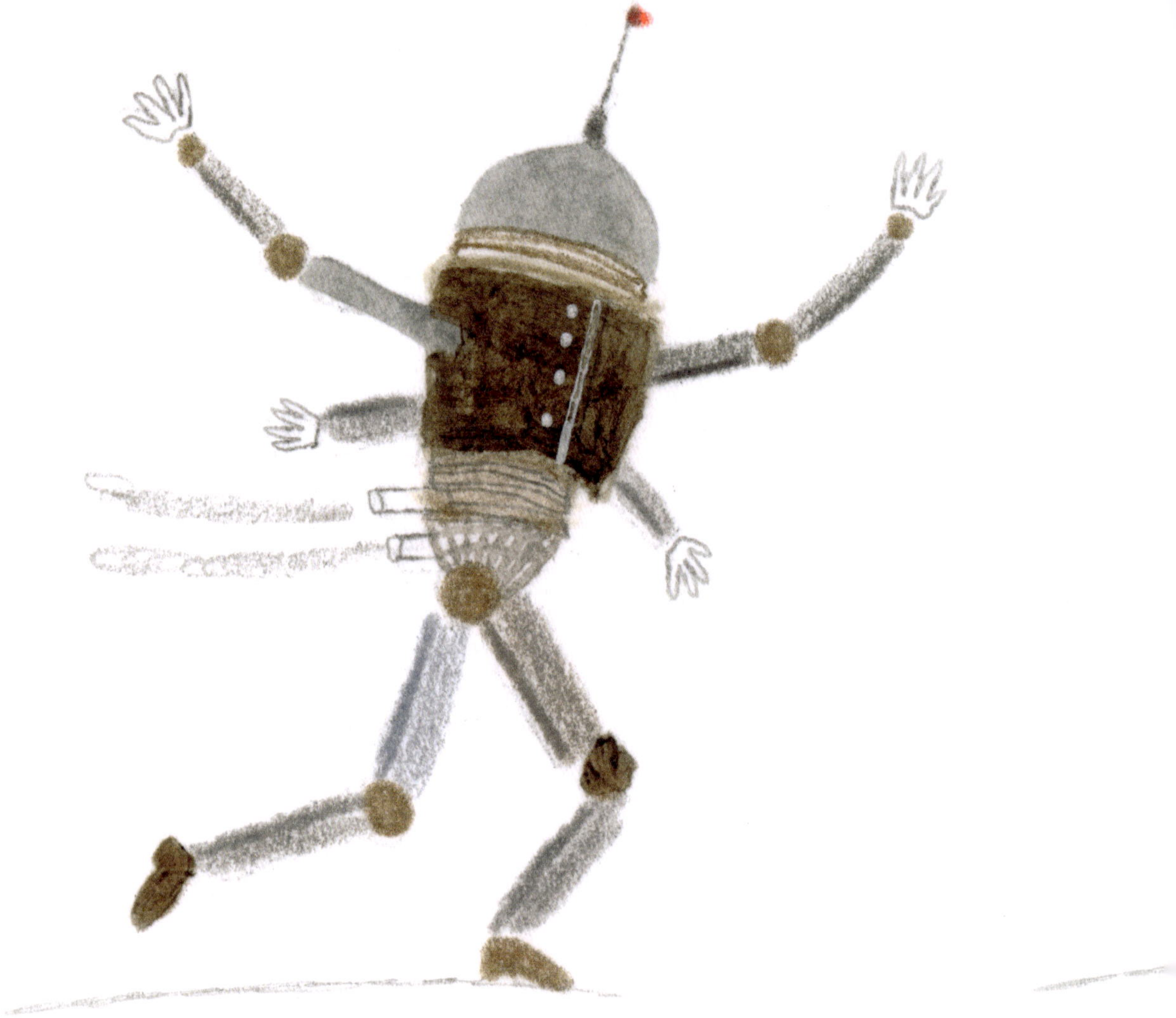

The mice are experienced
they've been in many tight spots!
Using Henry's equipment
they build a giant robot!

It chases Lion and Henry
with a whizz and a whirr
it attacks with lasers
zaps Henry's coat and Lion's fur!

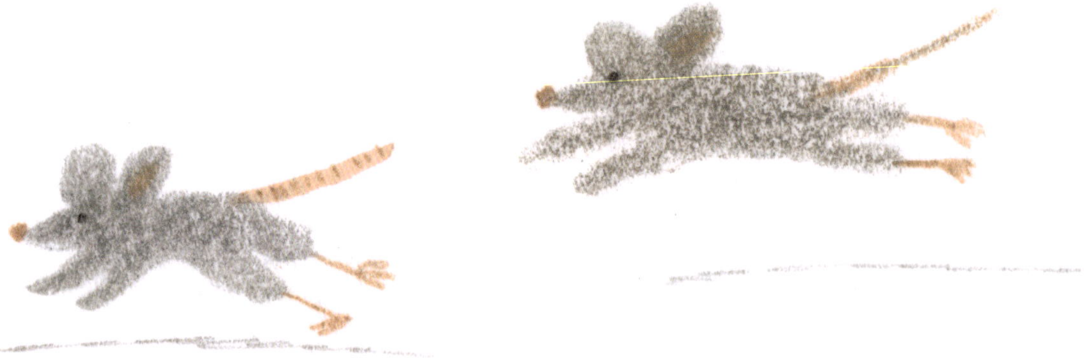

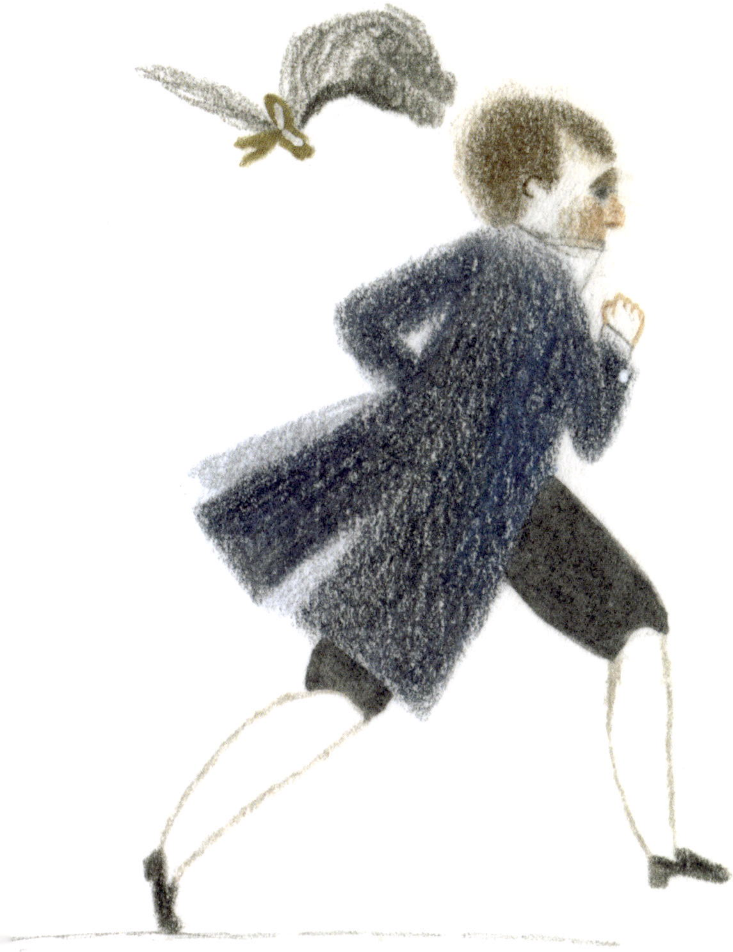

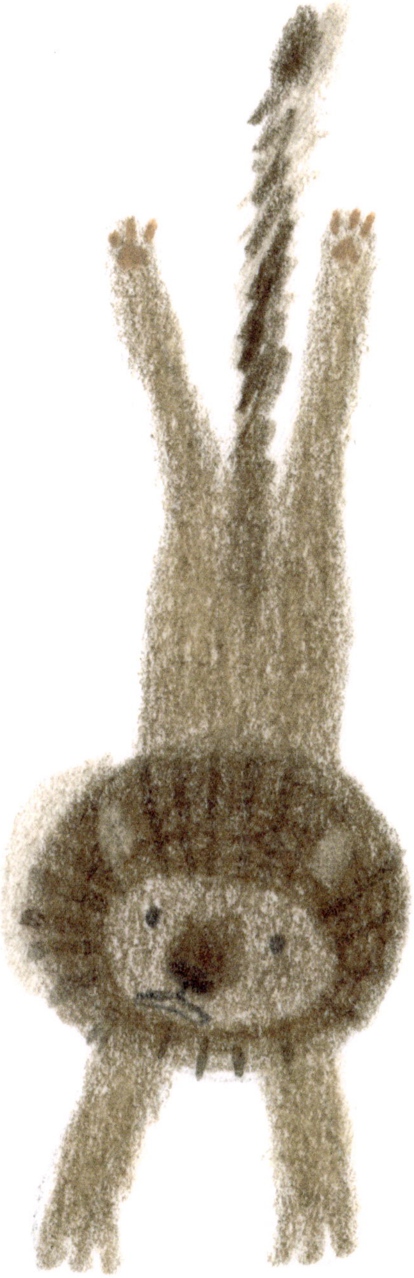

Little Lion finds courage,
decides he can't take any more.
He takes a deep lion breath
and gives a great big lion...

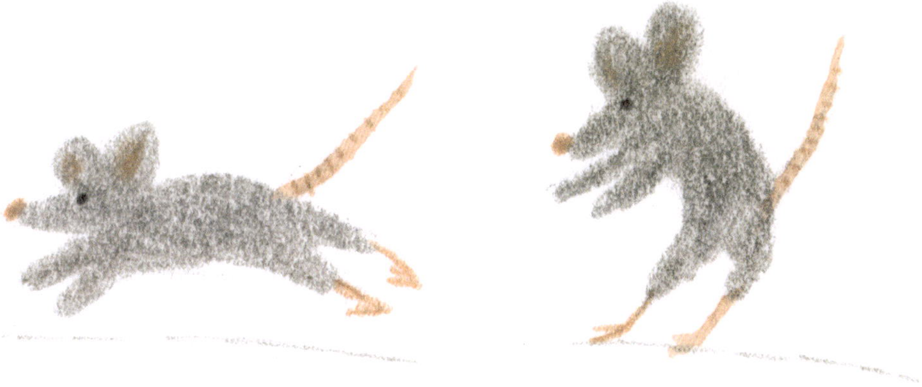

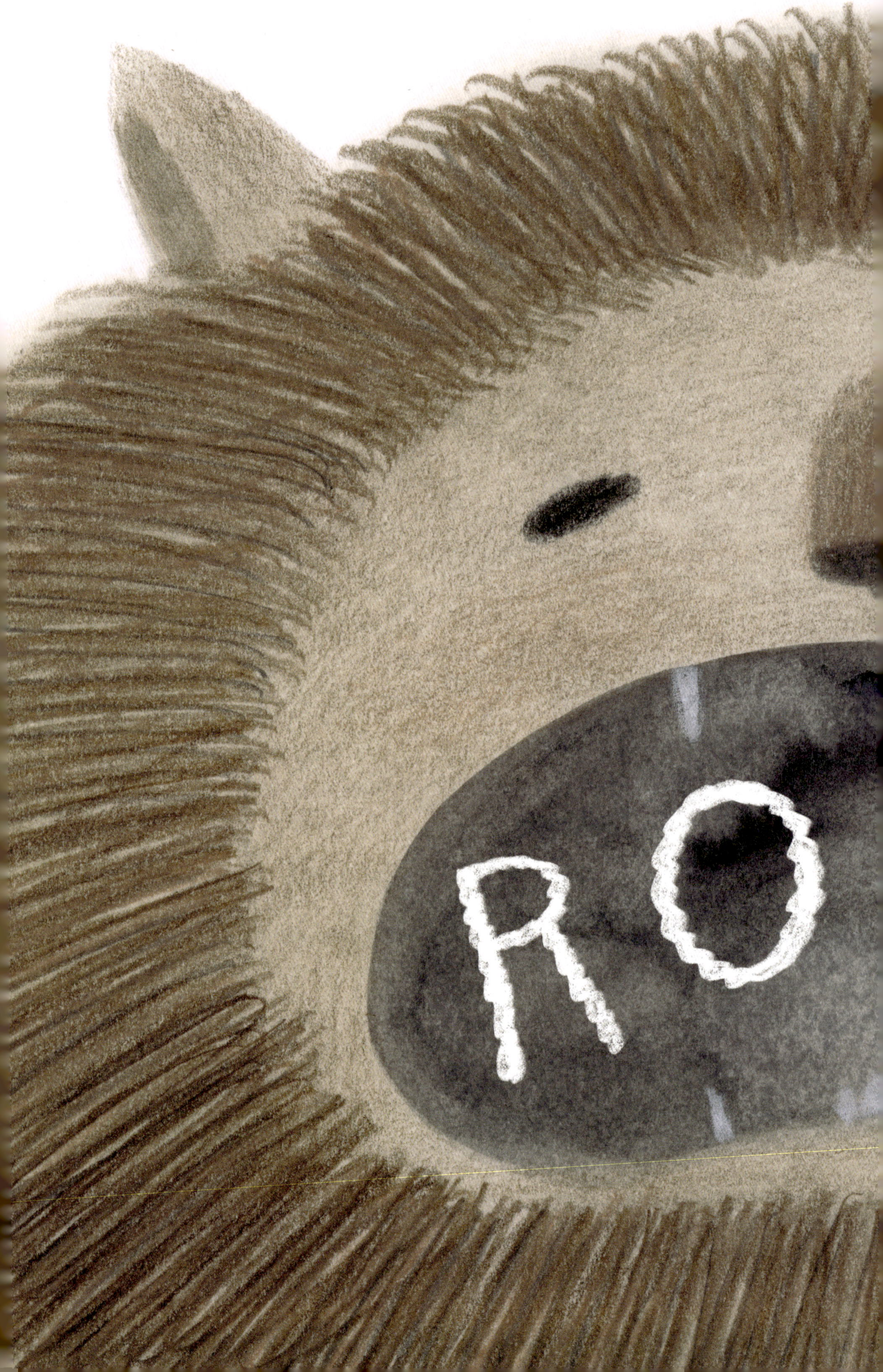
RO

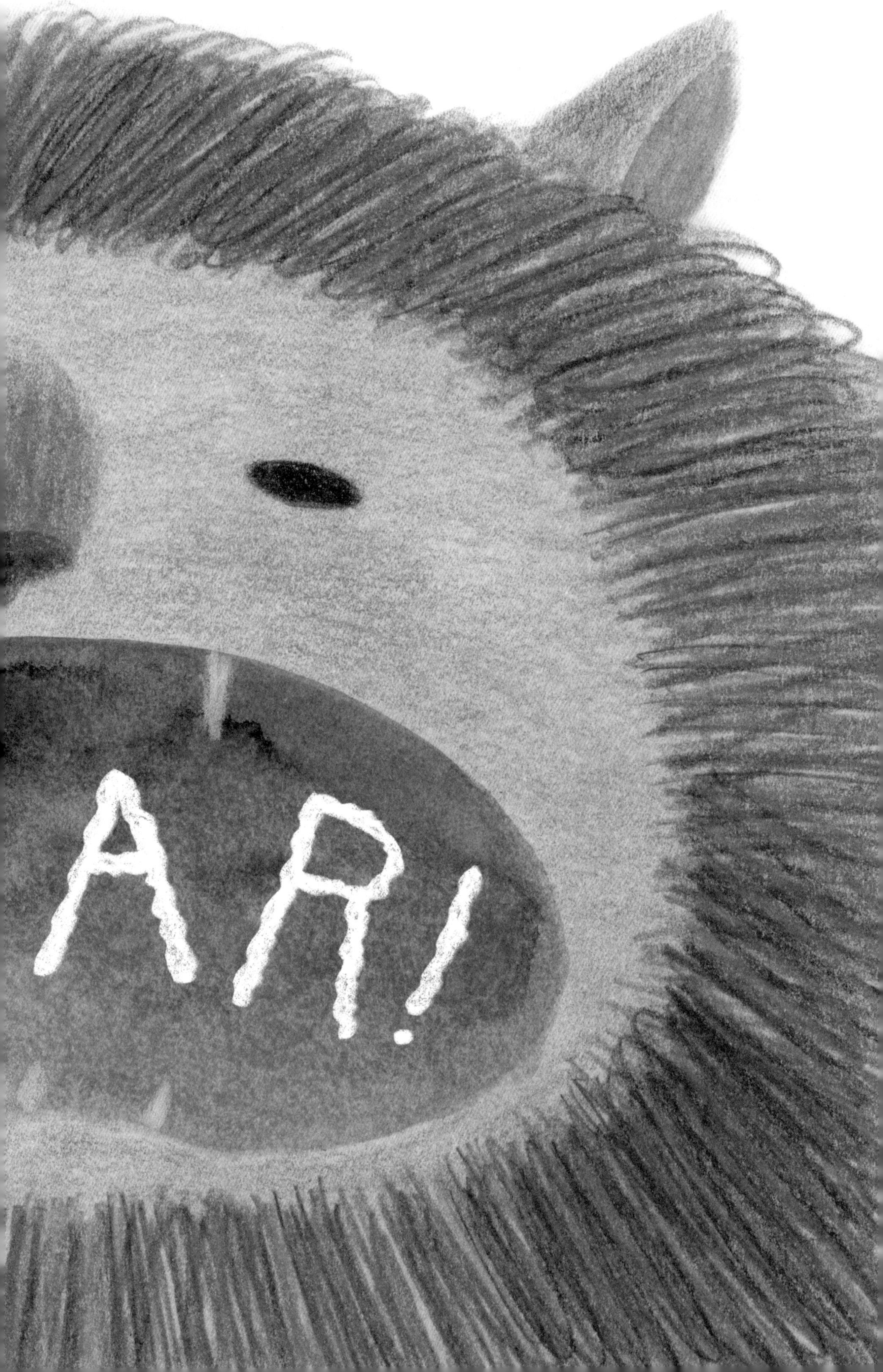
AR!

It echoes throughout Chatsworth,
tumbles Henry's globe to the ground!

"It must be very heavy
to make such a thudding sound!"

A new idea for an experiment
starts to bubble and take shape
Henry declares with an heroic air...

"I wish to work-out the world's weight!"

All are impressed
(including the mice)
they all agree to be friends,
they all decide to play nice!

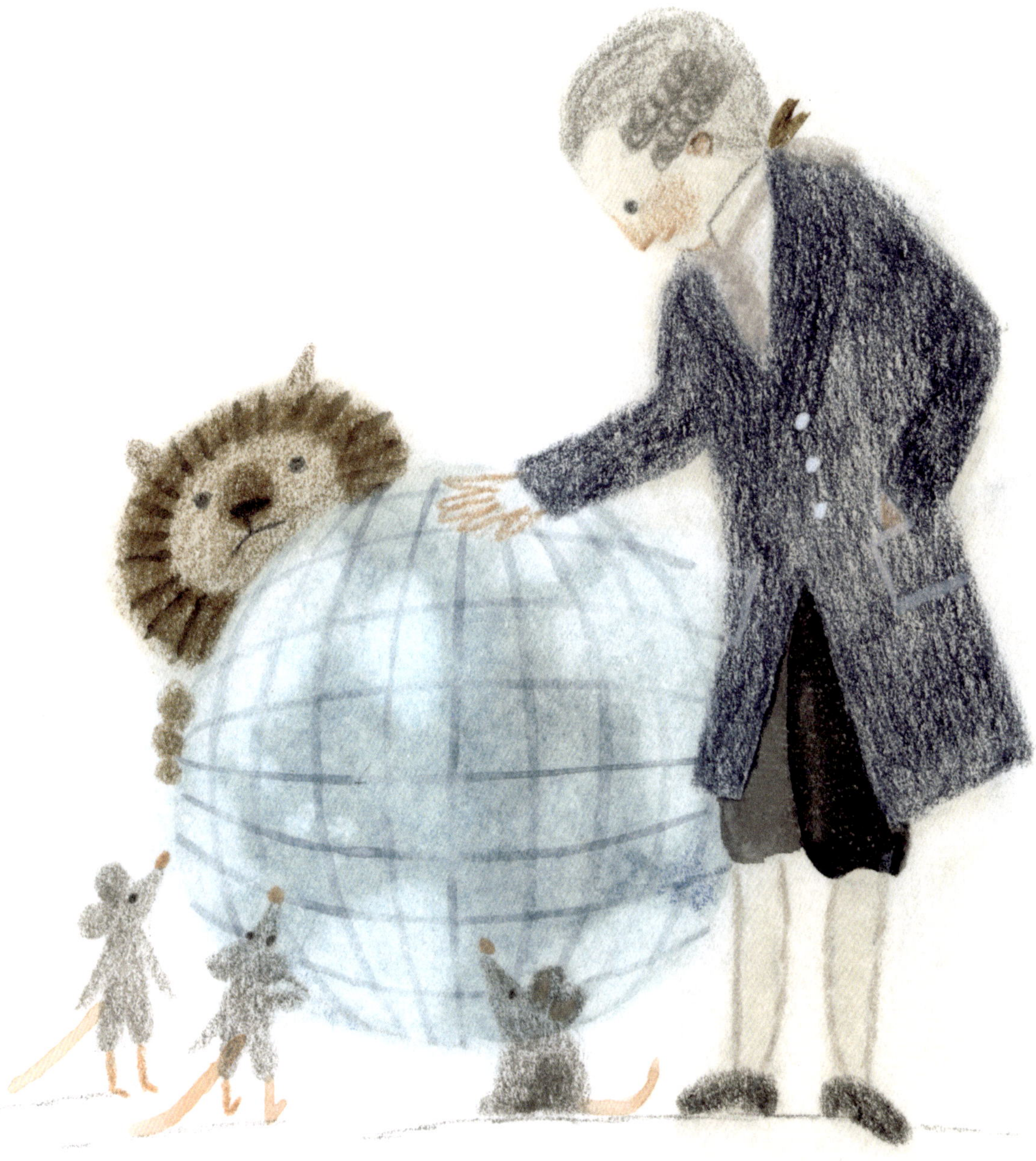

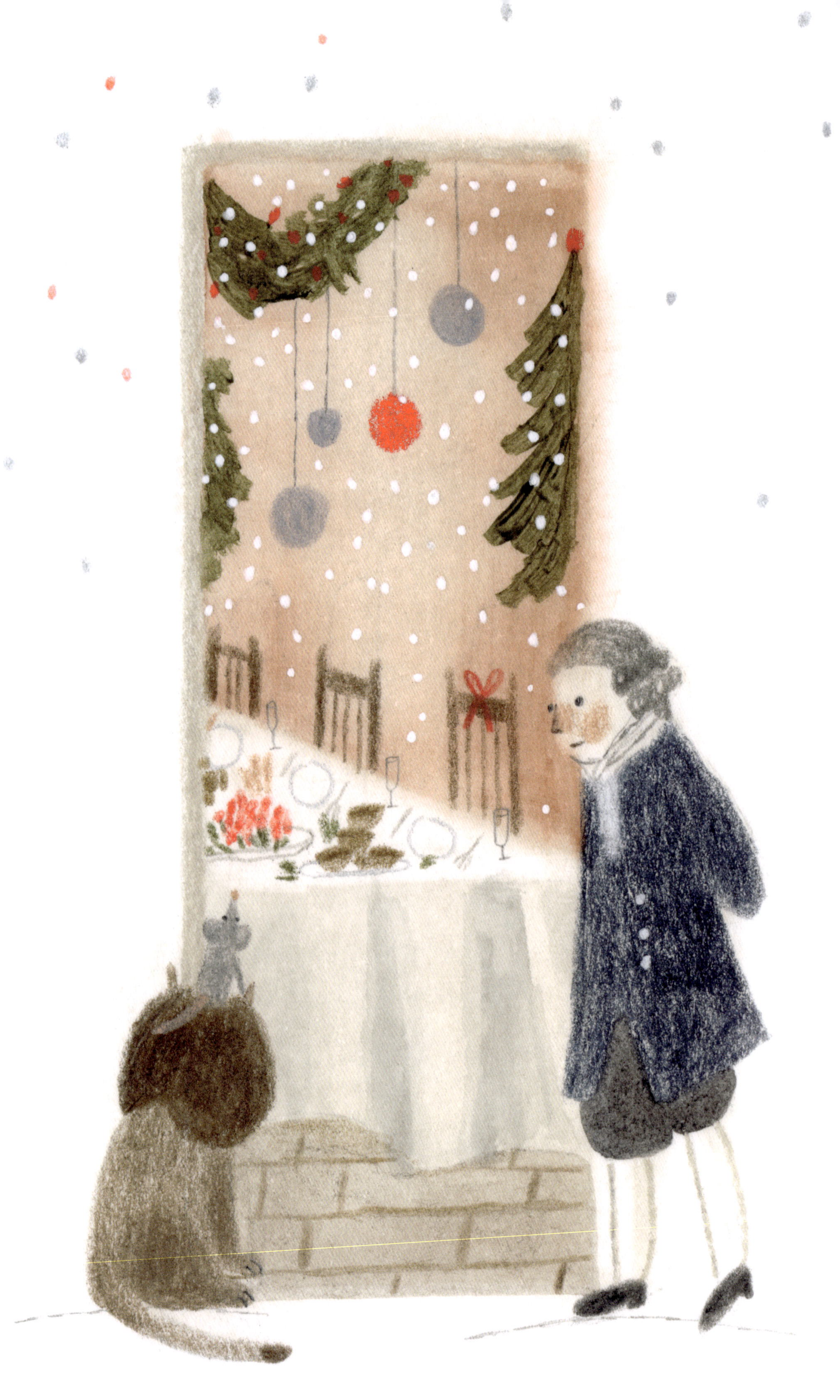

To the dining room they go,
all friends united,
where a festive feast is laid out
and everyone's invited.

There are steaming plum puddings
and sweet mince pies
there are mountains of veggies
piled incredibly high.

In come more guests
from all over the land
followed by a circus
and a booming brass band.

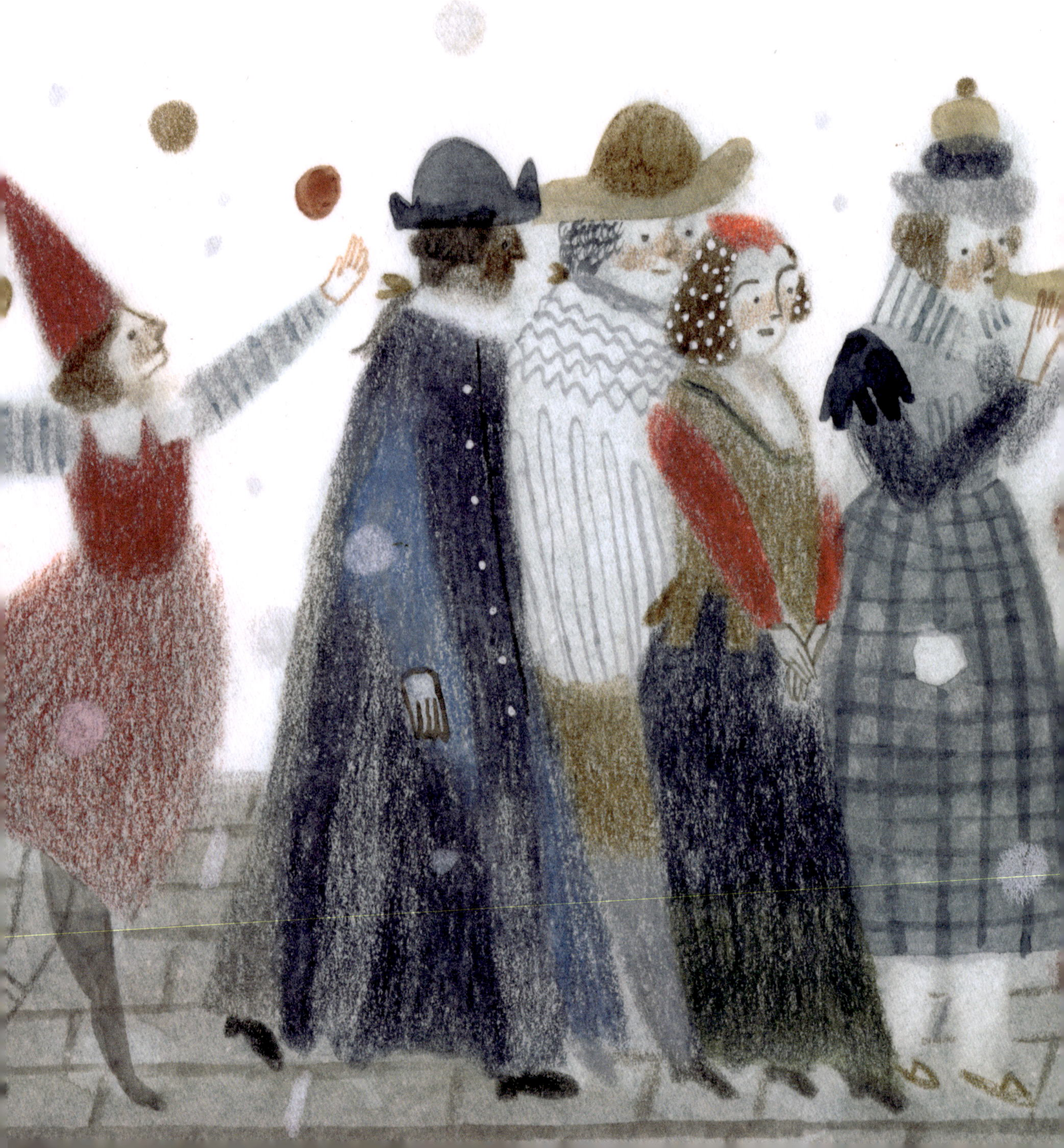

And then come the reindeer
with elves upon their backs,
then roll in the snow men
who start a snowball attack!

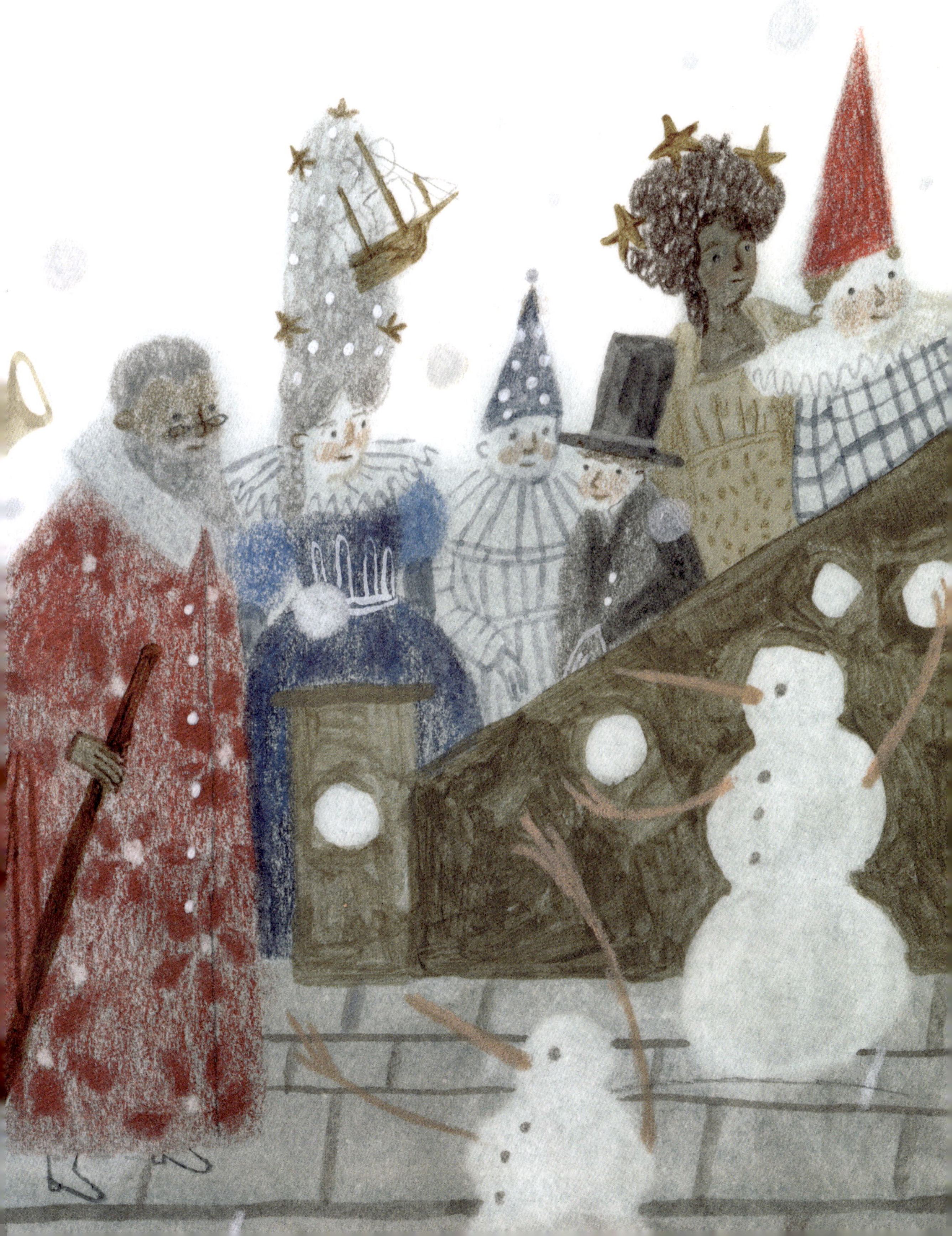

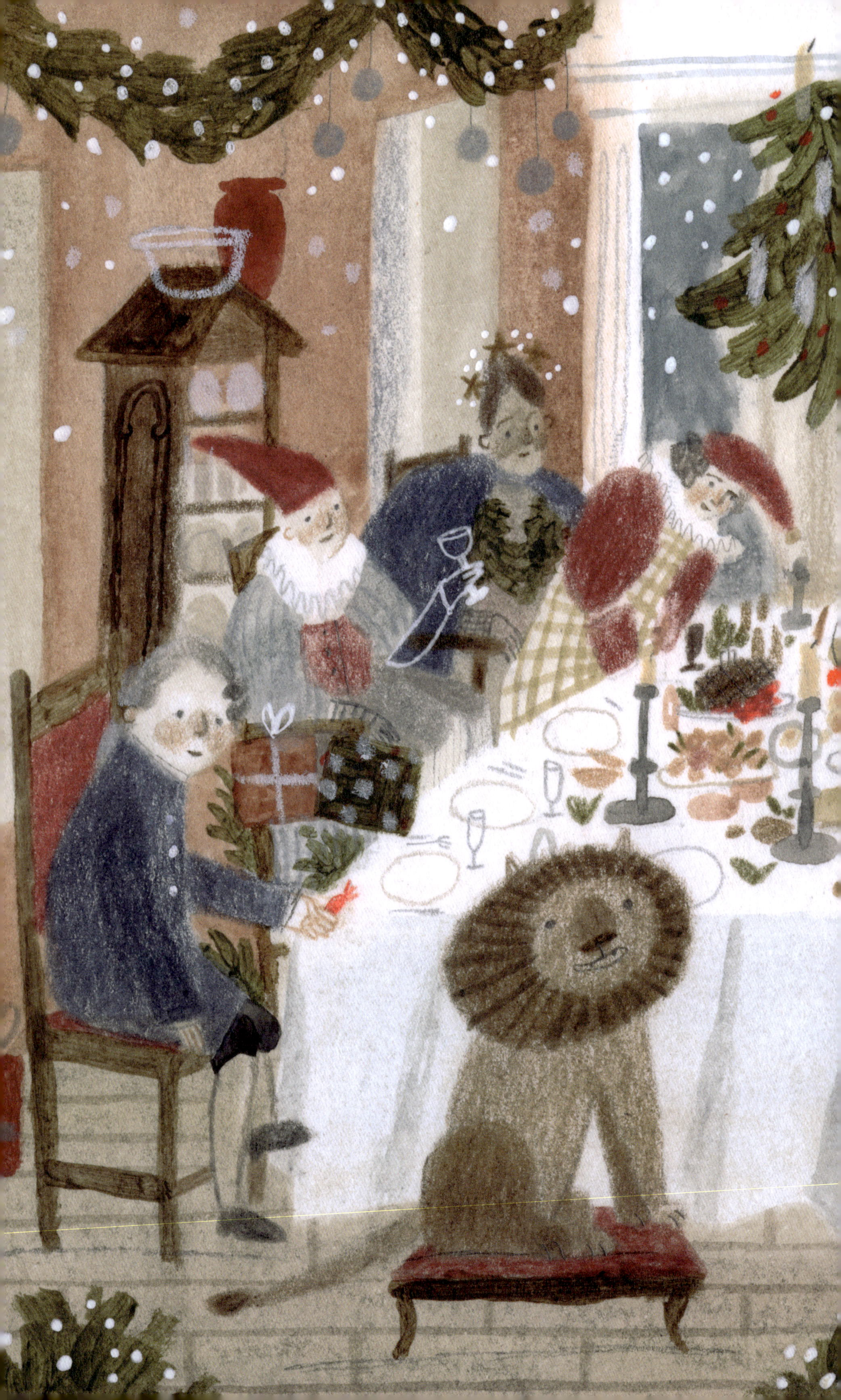

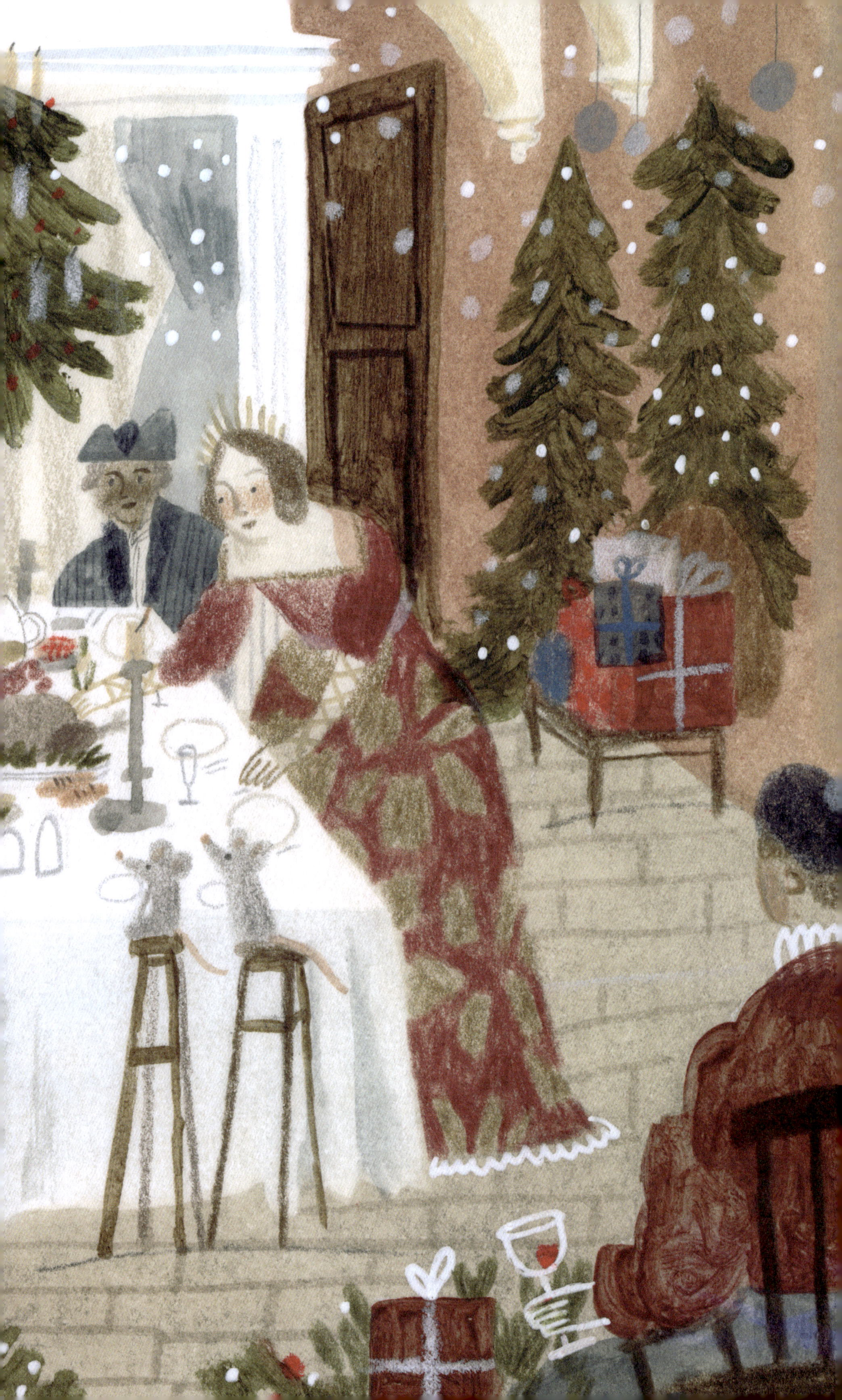

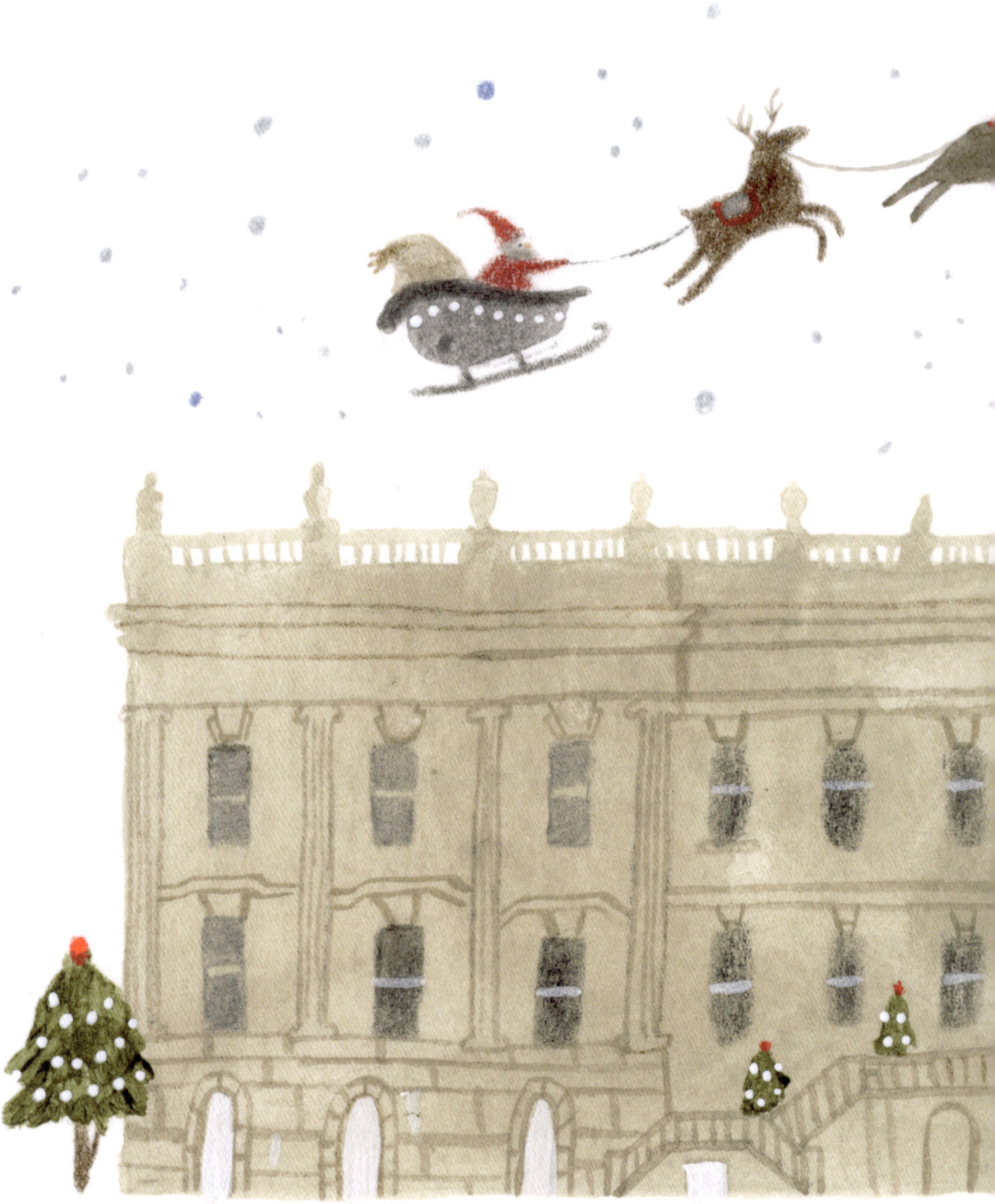

And everyone cheers
with a hip hip hooray!
As in slides Santa
riding high up on his sleigh.

And little Lion has grown
with joy and much grub!
Bigger than before
much bigger than a cub.

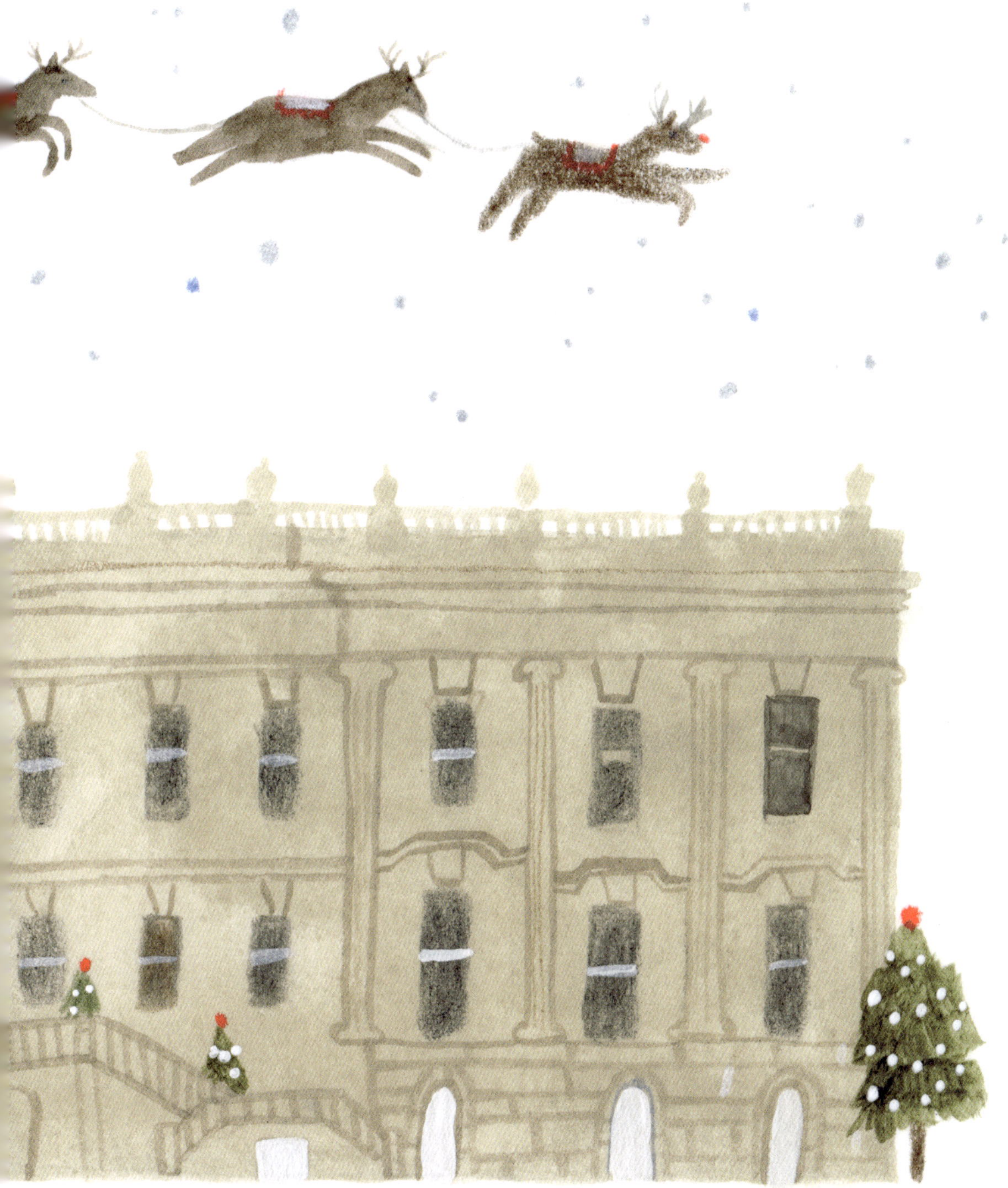

And Henry quickly makes a gift
for his new friendly beasty
to say thanks for the inspiration
to see how heavy the world might be!

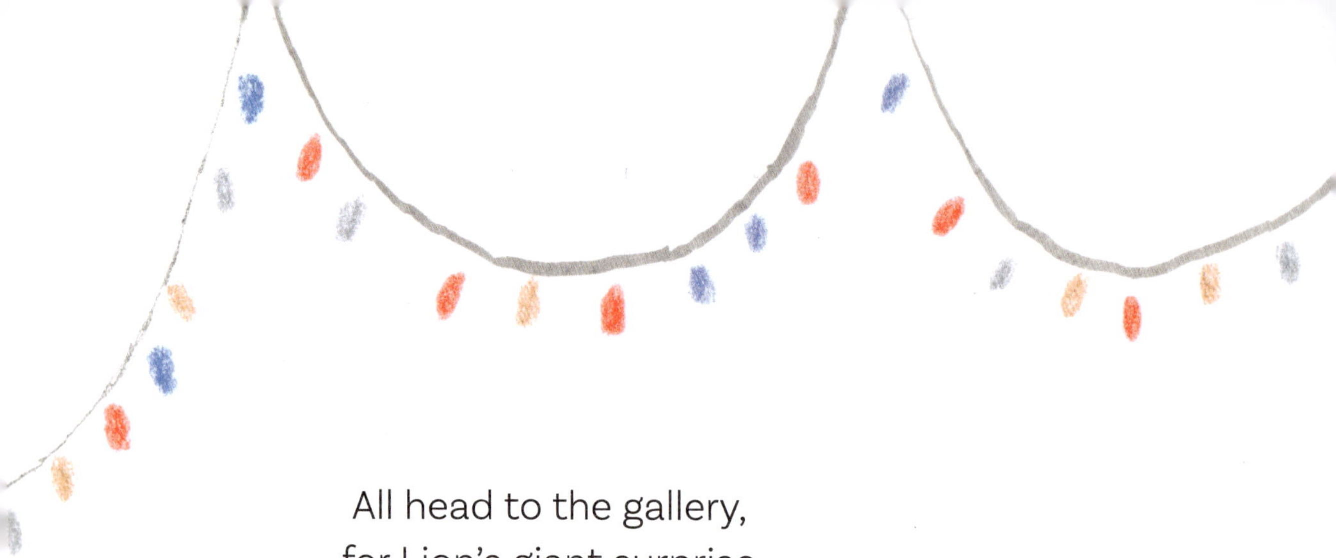

All head to the gallery,
for Lion's giant surprise
it's a statue of him!
Tears fill Lion's eyes!

The statue is massive
the statue is regal and grand -
wider than a car,
taller than a man!

It's as big as Lion's bliss.
It's as great as Lion's glee
and it's decorated too!
Lion feels so christmassy!

What a wonderful Christmas!
The world feels lighter than before
Let's all celebrate together
with a great big christmassy...

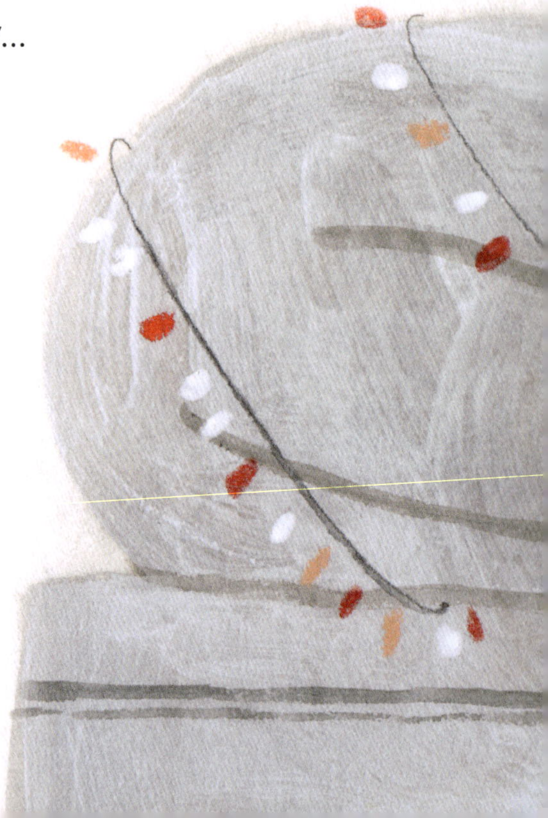

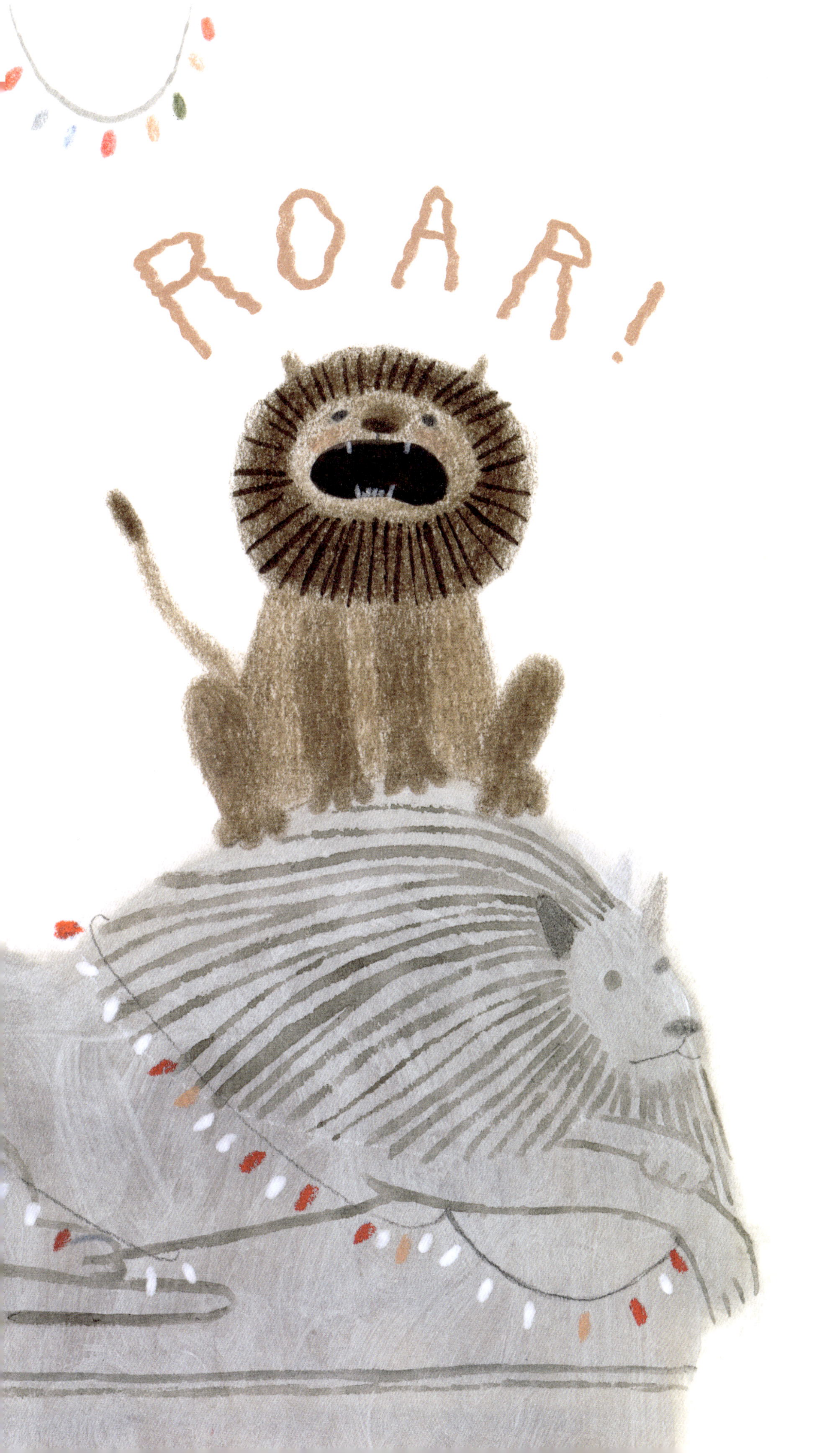
ROAR!

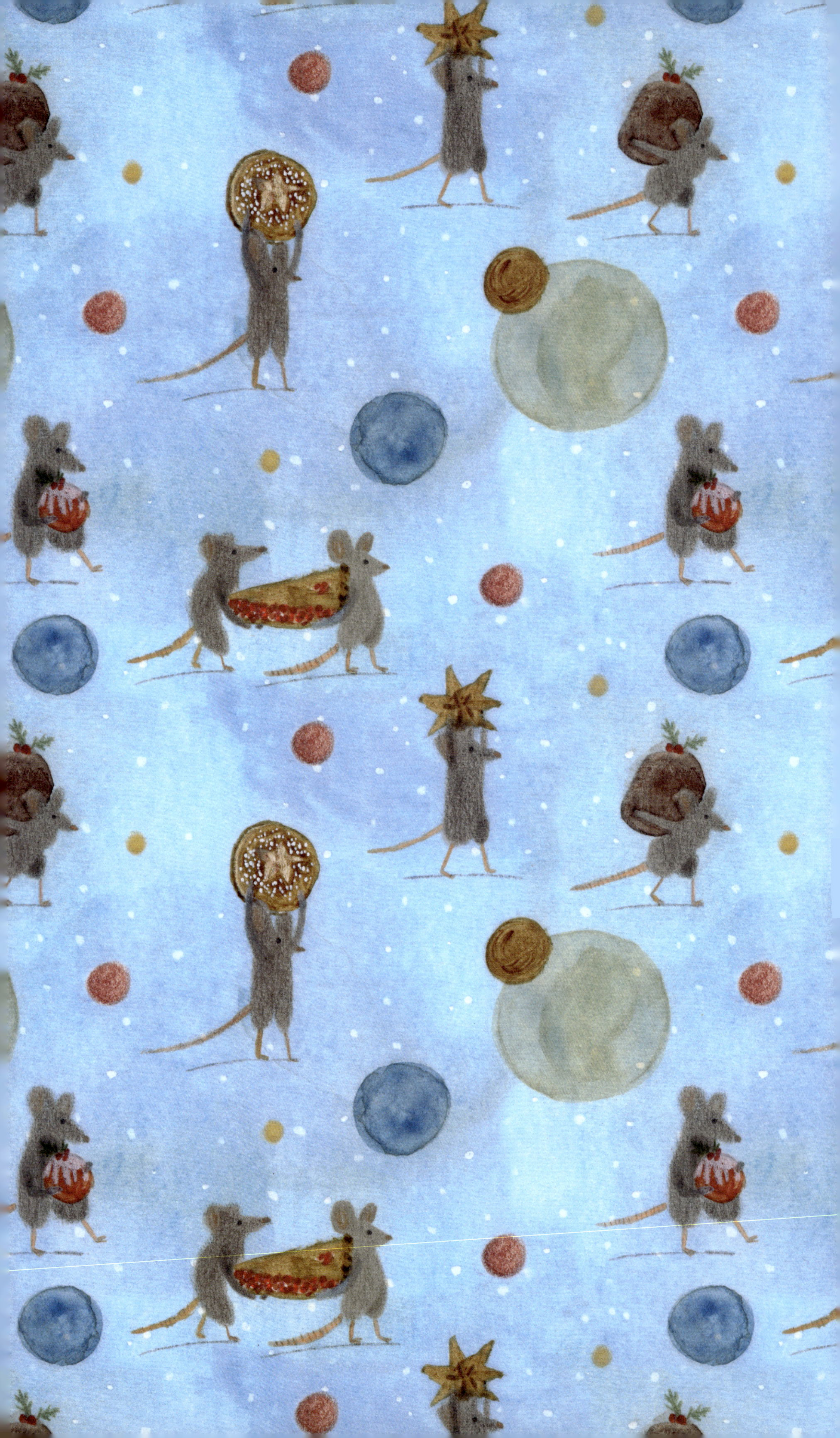